Legal Stuff, Cop
(You Know…The Stuff You Never Actually Read…)

TUESDAY'S CHILD NOVELS
PO BOX 584
WILBRAHAM, MA 01095
www.ZombiePoc.webs.com
www.TuesdaysChildNovel.com
TuesdaysChildNovel@Comcast.net

Copyright @2012 Carolyn Gibbs
All rights reserved. No part of this book may be reproduced, stored in a retrieval system, or transmitted in any form or by any means, electronic, mechanical, photocopying, recording, or any other method without the written permission of the author. **IF YOU DISREGARD THIS WARNING, THE FEDS OR THE ZOMBIES WILL ARRIVE AT YOUR DOOR…ARGUABLY THEY COULD BE ONE IN THE SAME.**

FIRST EDITION: 10/10/2012
ISBN-13: 978-1480063716
ISBN-10: 1480063711

Printed in the United States of America.

This book is a work of fiction! Fiction! FICTION! All names, characters, locations, and events are either the work of the author's imagination or are used fictitiously. I have no proof that Fort Knox is preparing for the Zombie Apocalypse. Additionally, any resemblance of characters to actual people, either living or dead, to locations, or to events, is purely in your head.

The cover art is also copyrighted, @2012 Patrick Ackerman, graphic designs. Used by license agreement.

Don't heist his work. To contact Patrick for your own projects, email him at: *121dl3y@gmail.com*

Dedication

TO EVERYONE

DETERMINED TO SURVIVE THE
ZOMBIE HORDE...

...AND TO THOSE OF YOU

DESTINED TO HELP THE ZOMBIES
SURVIVE...

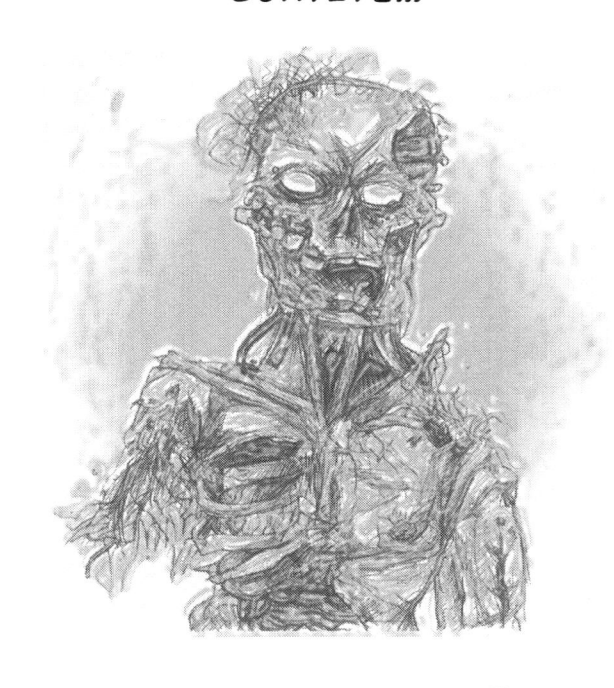

SURVIVE OR BE EATEN!

Surviving the Zombie 'Pocalypse

The Layman's Guide to Surviving the Zombie Apocalypse (And an Assortment of Other More Likely Disasters)

by Carolyn Gibbs

Table of Contents

Legal Stuff, Copyright Stuff, Contact Stuff... 1

Dedication 3

First things First 7

The Coming of the End 9

Water 13

Banding Together 22

Where to Make Your Stand 25

Ways to Dispatch Zombies 29

Let's Talk Zombies 33

Let's Talk Zombie Jokes 35

Food 36

But...There's No Food Left 43

The Go-Bag 45

Fire 48

Trees 53

Building Shelter 56

Who Owns the Stuff 61

Gasoline 63

Day to Day Living 65

The Family Pets 69

Crops 74

Toileting and Other Uncomfortable Conversations 79

When the World Goes Silent 81

Rules Of The Road 82

What To Do If a Zombie Is At Your Door 84

What To Do if the Zombie 'Pocalypse Hits While You Are At Work 85

Tons of Other Things 88

Which Disaster Shall It Be? 92

Steps You Can Take Now 93

Finally 95

A Disclaimer of Major Proportion 96

An Open Call 97

If You Enjoyed Zombie 'Pocalypse… 99

First things First

Who is this book for? Well it isn't for the folks who know the morphology of Zombie-ism, who have a couple AK-47's hiding under their floor boards so the Feds don't find them, or who have replaced several walls in their homes with number ten cans of dehydrated and freeze-dried foods. Those folks are already set for any disaster-event that may occur, ranging from an EM pulse to the Zombie Apocalypse.

This book is for those of you who don't know what an EM pulse is (Electro-Magnetic pulse), what a zombie looks like (you'll know him when he tries to bite your face off), or why you might want to prepare for the end of civilization as we know it (because some of us will survive, and none of us want to live like Neanderthals).

This is a Layman's book, to help those of you who don't possess the skills you'll need to survive.

The best part is that you can wait until the last minute…until the EM pulse takes out the lights or the zombie is politely knocking on your door. Be sure to use the handy Table of Contents in times of emergency so you don't waste any time flipping through the pages…a zombie isn't likely to wait too long while you try figure out how to kill him.

And as it turns out, you likely have waited almost to the bitter end…

The bad news, however, for those of you who put this on your Kindle, your PC, or your phone…the page numbers may not work at all, and the EM Pulse turned your nifty little electronic reading device into a paperweight anyway. You might want to invest in a copy of the paper version...

The Coming of the End

OK, the bacteria or virus escapes, and ten percent of the population develop a sudden urge to chow down on the first person they see.

If you see it happening, take note that the victim will slap, punch, and scream, but none of that will have any effect whatsoever. They'll get bitten or scratched, and they in turn will become a zombie.

The initial ten percent infected pass the virus along until the zombified outnumber the living 9 to 1. Are you reading this in a public place? Look around the room, the coffee shop, the doctor's office...most of those people are already doomed. Distance yourself from them now.

Now consider this...the initial infection was the result of some biological accident. The first zombie didn't get bitten or scratched...he breathed in or ingested the virus.

That means you breathed it in, too. Should Uncle Joe have a heart attack and die during your travels, don't leave him in the backseat until you find a nice place to bury him. Stop the car. If he just died, get him out of the car. If he died five minutes ago, then you need to get out of the vehicle because zombification is under way. You don't want him lunging over the seat to taste your earlobes while you're driving.

If the escaped bacteria or virus doesn't cause Zombie-ism, then it's the old-fashioned type of biological...like Ebola, Anthrax, or Small Pox. It won't matter to you whether it was a bacteria or a virus, you'll just be happy that no one wants to lunch on your gizzards.

On the other hand, you should worry about catching the infection. Some infections will travel by contact, others by air, and others by interaction with contaminated body fluids or tissues. That being said don't play with any lungs you find lying in the street. And stay away from anyone who is obviously sick. If a dose of humanity forces you to try to save them, gown up. Face mask, gloves, smock…leave nothing to chance.

Next up…a nuclear accident or attack. You can't hide from the nuclear fallout, though you can iodine yourself and try to ward off the effects of radiation on your thyroid.

Another possibility is an Electro-Magnetic Pulse. An EM pulse takes out all electrical activity. Your house, your neighbors, the town…all remain. But the support structure is trash. Cars, phones, computers, TVs, refrigerated tractor trailers that haul our food from one end of the country to another…yeah, none of that works. Let's hope Stephen King still has a typewriter to churn out those heart-stoppers.

Finally, some natural disaster could befall us, like a meteor taking out Great Britain. Gosh dang it—no more bangers and mash. A global killer pretty much ends the discussion, but say the meteor that squishes our Brit cousins is only a half-mile wide. It's going to do some serious damage to the impact site and a large distance out, and that tidal wave it creates will hit the east coast of the USA.

After the initial impact, it kicks up a dust cloud that eventually circles the globe. Guess what…you can't grow crops in the dark and you can't breathe mud. No grains for feed animals, no burgers and pork chops for people…mass death.

Lest you dismiss meteors as the stuff of science fiction, consider that a nuclear cloud can do the same thing, as can volcanic ash.

The bottom line is that a disaster of global magnitude, or even just national scope, will disrupt the lives of everyone caught in the affected area. Shipping lanes close, herds and crops die in the fields, and chaos reigns as people realize rather quickly that they can no longer jog down to the local Publix for a loaf of bread and a bottle of sunscreen.

Looting prevails, and the chaos grows. The stores empty first. Average citizens are pushed to join criminals in the shopping centers. You might think you can tell the difference between the two...after all, the guy with the ninety-four inch flat screen TV has to be a criminal, no? Perhaps, but watch yourself because even an otherwise law-abiding citizen will mug you for the last dozen eggs. After all, whose family is more important...yours or his? Depends on who you are, doesn't it?

Last October, a freak snowstorm dropped more than two feet of snow in some places of New England. Some of us will always refer to it as the Halloween storm. Trees came down and with them power lines...we were effectively trapped in our homes, forced to survive with only what we had on hand.

A lot of folks have probably a week's worth of food in the house at any given time. Three days after the snowfall the roads had been cleared, albeit only one lane in many places, and folks were able to get to the stores. How much worse would the storm have been if the weight of the snow had taken down the roof of the public works building, trapping the plows and municipal trucks inside? How would those of us stuck in our homes have gotten out? I've got a chainsaw, but it certainly will not ever be able to get through a one-hundred-year-old oak.

Self-sufficiency is the best option. Plan for something…anything. Will it be the Zombie 'Pocalypse, a meteor, or an economic disaster? Doesn't matter. There are some survival preparations that meet at least a few criteria for all emergencies.

Think of it this way. You plan for parties all the time, stocking in extra food and necessities. Do the same for your survival. You can start now, or you can wait until the emergency occurs. But if you wait, you will need to wade into the fray to get yourself some supplies.

Water

OK, so you all know you need water. You probably know that you can't just belly-up to a river and drink until your thirst is slaked...they do that in the movies without any concern, but if you do it you will end up with worms or worse, parasites crapped out of fish and bears and raccoons. Without access to a medical professional, you will suffer greatly before you die. You'll probably throw yourself in front of the first zombie you see just to get it over with.

Of course, if you are a medical professional, have at it.

For the rest of you, there are decisions to make, and all your decisions will circle around the disaster like sharks on a surfer with razor burn:

- If you leave the house you are a target, a moving target perhaps but you might as well ring the dinner bell for the hungry undead. It will only be a matter of time before one of them sees you, follows you, and eats you.
- If you don't leave the house, you will not have enough supplies to survive long term.

That said, we've already established that you didn't prepare for 1999 (some thought that was code for the beginning of the Devil's reign), Y2K (the change of centuries), or 2012 (the end of the Mayan calendar and supposedly the end of time).

You didn't prepare for Swine Flu, Bird Flu, West Nile Virus, or the Epidemic of Ingrown Toenails. You have nothing in your homes to combat food shortages, electricity outages, epidemics, insolvency of the American dollar, or those pesky zombies.

Leaving your house will be required. Unfortunately, the minute you step out the door you not only open yourself up to the possibility of becoming someone else's dinner or ending up with an incurable disease, you also open yourself up for human discovery.

Much as you might be interested in banding together with other humans for mutual survival, others may not be so interested…they may just want your supplies. Once you're visible, even the living will follow you home, if only to boost your hard-earned resources. After all, it'll be easier to steal from a secluded survivor than to face the zombie horde that might be sludging around the local grocery store.

You must learn to identify the good, the bad, and the ugly, and to defend yourself from the latter two.

Back to water. Yes, you need it. Lots of it. Clean is better, but dirty can be cleaned. You need it for drinking, cooking, watering your crops and animals, and washing.

What should you wash? Your body and your clothes. No…don't wash the car. Don't wash the house. Don't wash the dog unless he gets skunked. You also don't need to bathe daily, but you do need to keep your hands clean so you don't accidentally ingest something toxic or parasitic.

If you're lucky enough to live near a store that hasn't been ransacked by survivors, nab all the bottled beverages, especially the water, and save it for drinking.

If you don't happen to live in Aisle 8 of Stop & Shop, then you will have to gather water from a fresh water source...brook, stream, river, pond, lake, reservoir, or even a bog.

What you need for gathering water:

- The fresh water source
- A rope (optional)
- A bucket
- A tank (or other large storage container)
- A truck (or other suitable vehicle)

What you need for purifying water:

- The water
- Towels or tee shirts
- A fire
- Two pots, more if available
- Jars or jugs for storing the water
- Unscented Bleach (do not use color-safe bleach or bleaches with additional chemicals....you're not doing laundry here...you need to be able to drink the water when you're done)

What to do:

- If the fresh water source is dangerous to reach or approach, as in a fast-moving river or at the bottom of a cliff, then tie the rope on the bucket handle and toss it in. You can also use this method if you simply don't want to get wet...after all, it will be harder to run from zombies if you are weighed down by ten extra pounds of water in your pants and shoes.
- Empty your full water bucket into the larger storage container. This larger container needs to be in your

vehicle already. Water is heavy...a single gallon weighs just over eight pounds. By the time you've hauled ten buckets of water out of the nearest river, you've got nearly eighty-five pounds on your hands...be sure your storage tank is already in the truck.

- Water gathered this way must be purified. Since you likely have no chemical purifiers on hand, boiling becomes your only choice. It's also the most reliable...kudos to you for not stocking up on iodine pills. Start by straining it through the towels or tee shirts into a pot. This will remove excess debris. Let it sit for a half-an-hour and repeat the straining if necessary.
- Bring the water to a rolling boil. The time varies depending on your altitude above sea-level...skip the guessing and boil your water for five minutes.
- This first batch of water will be lost to disinfecting the jars and jugs in which you will store future batches. Don't use milk jugs. Wash the jugs or jars in soap and water, and then completely submerge them in a bleach-water solution for at least fifteen seconds. Rinse them in a weaker bleach-water solution.
- Subsequent batches will have to cool before you can pour them into these disinfected jars and jugs. As you get used to the process, you will be able to multi-task but for now just concentrate on getting it right.
- Pour the cooled water into the prepared jugs. If you plan on drinking it all today, you don't need to worry about long-term storage. However, if you are preparing your long-term stores, one more step preserves your water for six months. Be sure to date the bottles.

- Liquid bleach in your purified water lets you keep it longer. Check the Numbers section below for the amount of bleach to add to each jug.
- DO NOT TOUCH the rim of the jar or the inside of the cap…do not contaminate the water you just worked so hard to clean.

Drinking Bleach Water

Yeah, it could taste funny. Here's the kicker…if you can't smell a little chlorine, it means that all the chlorine was used up fighting bacteria. If you do smell a little chlorine, then there's plenty of chlorine still left to fight bugs.

What does that mean? Can I drink it or not? If it doesn't smell a little chlorine, I'd be tempted to boil it again. If I had plenty of water on hand, I'd just use it for washing bodies or clothes.

Don't expect stored water to be refreshing. It's just hydration. If it tastes too bad for your liking, try adding a dash of salt. If it still isn't tasty, add some powdered drink mix to it.

And do yourself another favor…despite how manly it looks or how much time it takes to needlessly pour a beverage into a glass, don't drink from the bottle. Once your lips touch that jar, you've introduced bacteria. From that instant, you have just twenty-four hours to finish it before those bacteria multiply to the point of making you ill. Think about how you'll run away from zombies while fighting diarrhea and vomiting.

The Numbers:

- Bleach-water solution for disinfecting jars with a 6% unscented chlorine bleach:
    - 4 teaspoons per gallon
    - 1 teaspoon per quart
- Bleach for water storage using a 4-6% unscented chlorine bleach:
    - 8 drops per gallon
    - 4 drops per half-gallon
    - 2 drops per quart
- Bleach for water storage using a 1% unscented chlorine bleach:
    - 40 drops per gallon
    - 20 drops per half-gallon
    - 10 drops per quart
- Bleach for water storage using a 7-10% unscented chlorine bleach:
    - 4 drops per gallon
    - 2 drops per half-gallon
    - 1 drops per quart
- The average person should drink ½ gallon of water per day.
- The average person busting their butt surviving may need four times that or more.
- The average person is accustomed to using eighty plus gallons per day, most of it going to toilet flushing and showering.

One of your big challenges will be learning how to utilize your water more efficiently. You're used to turning a spigot and having a never-ending flow of fresh, mostly clean water. Once you have to purify it yourself, you'll learn quickly not to pour that half-empty glass down the sink or spend twenty minutes standing in the shower, watching the transparent blood of life swirl down the drain.

You'll also adopt clever ways for reusing and recycling water. A basin in the sink can be used to catch hand-washing water which can then be used for watering crops. Ditto for tub water and laundry water. Water barrels attached to your downspouts will gather water close to home, saving you trips down to the river. An added tip for those rain barrels is also the addition of bleach, which will keep down mosquitos.

Another issue to consider is where you live. Temperate zones may not have to worry about storing water through the winter...you will likely have access to fresh, flowing water on a daily basis until eternity arrives.

Northern areas with a regular winter will lose the water sources shortly after the temperature dips toward freezing. Desert regions will get to watch the water evaporate day by day until river and streambeds have completely dried up. And all this will happen without effecting zombies, viruses, or magnetic pulses at all.

To compensate for the variability of your water supply, calculate how much time you have left until your water supply becomes inaccessible. Divide that number into the amount of water you need to survive your frozen or dry period. That is the number of extra gallons, per person, that you must prepare and put away daily if you are to survive the winter.

Example: You expect your water source will freeze in December and not thaw until sometime in April...5 months or

150 days. It is now September 1. September 1 to November 31 gives 3 months or 90 days until your water is frozen and becomes a highway for zombies. 150/90 = 1.67. Round it and prepare 2 gallons of water per day per person that you will put aside. Date all bottles and use the oldest first.

Those living in frozen zones who don't have sufficient time to prepare these long-term stores will have to be able to break through the ice...you have to get to the water of the local river or pond. Pick, axe, auger, chain saw...you'll need something to break through. You can always just cut out blocks of ice and thaw it for water...eight pounds of ice will yield nearly one gallon of water.

Unfortunately, for those of you living in arid regions...if you don't store up water before your river dries for the season, kiss your butt goodbye. On the bright side, you'll be dead before the zombies find you.

"Wait...you didn't tell me why I can't just turn on the tap?"

Because without electricity your artesian or shallow well has no way to pump water into your house. Because without people monitoring the pressure via equipment run on electricity, the pressure in the city water pipes will drop and no water will come out of those pipes in your house.

Because the only way you'll experience anything remotely similar to the convenience of modern water distribution systems is if you happen to live underneath a water tower or other similar gravity fed supply.

If, however, you have the skill and equipment, you can always dig a well and install either a hand pump or a bucket and rope system. The bottom line, however, is that you will have to work for your water from now on.

Banding Together

To Band or Not To Band...that is the question.

Solitude allows you to move quickly, at a moment's notice, without worrying about Uncle Joe's wheelchair, Aunt Gertrude's gout, or if your entire party has the same game plan in mind. Are you all heading in the same direction, or are you breaking up and meeting somewhere? Was it McDonald's, or was it Macy's? Damn, I don't remember where we're going!

Living alone allows you to get in and out of a store, grabbing a bag of chips before the zombies finishing off the butcher figure out there's fresh meat in Aisle 6. Unfortunately, it means there's no one to cover your back so the zombies chowing down on the baker can sneak up behind you.

One person cannot adequately protect a large structure, cannot take some target practice on the advancing horde *and* look for an escape route at the same time. Sure you can move quickly, but while you're racing around the house looking for a door that doesn't have zombies on the other side, your supplies, go-bag (more on that later), and the rest of your ammo get left behind.

Banding together, then, seems to be the solution. A couple hundred people will have no trouble fending off small bands of mindless automatons, finding a free escape route, gathering up the supplies, and hitting the road in a convoy that will easily crush any lone zombie encountered on the street.

Just one problem…while the vanguard actually gets away, the rear of the troop will be overrun…they'll be sticking around for dinner…and breakfast…and lunch…

Anyway, a band too big is just as dangerous as a band too small. So, what is the optimum number? Depends on what you're doing…staying in or moving out.

If you're staying in, you need someone to monitor every outside wall of the building, preferably from a high spot. A four-sided house needs a person monitoring each side, and someone to spell them every two to four hours. The first four need to sleep, so you need another four to be working, boiling water, reloading bullets, sharpening stakes.

You're up to twelve, leaving you fairly mobile in case of emergency. Better get along well with these folks because if you happen to be trapped in a two-room cape, you'll be falling all over each other.

If you're bugging out, heading to Fort Knox maybe because you heard from a passing stranger that all the survivors were meeting up there, the same rules apply. You need a mobile force with enough bodies to protect the troop as you move, and small enough that neither the front nor rear gets so far away from the rest of the band that it looks like the baby gazelle at the end of the herd.

How many? This is a major judgment call. Fifteen to twenty is a decent number, but neither can you turn someone away if they happen to be number twenty-one. Beef up your security, move in as few vehicles as possible, and make sure each car or truck has sufficient weaponry should the need arise.

If the world becomes zombified while you're at your annual family picnic and you find yourself with a couple hundred close and distant relatives, you will have to decide if you're sticking together or not. You have the option to build walls, fortify your shelter, and prepare to weather the storm in place. Or you might decide to break into smaller groups and seek already fortified locales. Of course, if you don't like your close and distant relatives, you could always feed them to the zombies...provided they don't have the same in mind for you.

Where to Make Your Stand

So, you've decided whether you're staying in place or moving around. Either way, you'll need a place to make your stand. Staying in place is obvious...you need a place in which you can take refuge. But even if you're moving, you need a safe zone for your overnight stays.

If you happen to find a twelve-foot concrete wall surrounding a property and it includes a heavy, steel gate across the driveway, then yeah! Stay there. Cover over that gate so the casual passerby zombie won't see you and decide to invite the rest of his friends for dinner. Become your own gated community, and use the wall to your advantage. You can even reduce the number of guards because the wall will prevent any sneak attacks.

Should you find a small, well-fortified gated community, you can spread out a little. But if you live in that two-room cape...yeah, get out now. Find something defensible. Anything surrounded by a solid fence will do. Keep in mind that a stockade fence will not hold up to the pressing of flesh against it, a shrub fence does nothing to save your butt, and a chain link fence lets the zombies drool while they figure out how to get through to the zoo animals inside...namely you.

What if you can't find a twelve-foot concrete wall? Use some discretion. Here's some specific do's and don'ts regarding taking over buildings:

Hospital: great for raiding the pharmacy, but too large to defend.

Grocery store: that's where the food is, but it's too large to defend *and* those glass windows let all the zombies see inside.

Convenience Stores: See Grocery store above. If it has windows only along the top of the walls, make that place yours.

Pharmacy: See Hospital above. If you find a small-town, Mom-n-Pop Pharmacy, it will be easier to defend and will likely not have large, glass windows. It will also have some food, probably just chips and the like, but it'll keep you alive.

Gas station: Ah, here's something…small building, probably has a little convenience store, and with a repair bay or two, you can bring your escape vehicles right inside.

Police station: Not a bad choice…there's weapons, maybe even a stale donut. Stay away from the cells though. Do not lock yourself in there thinking it'll keep you safe from zombies. It won't.

Library: A solid, brick structure is always a comfort. Multiple floors give you a retreat option. And the books will give you some old-fashioned paper knowledge in case you forget to boil your water and have to self-treat for worms. Plus, the tax code will make great kindling.

Bank: The vault will certainly keep zombies out. It'll also keep air out. Good news, though…once you've suffocated, the zombies will go away.

Bars: Small, dark, no big windows…and alcohol for all of your medicinal needs. Limited escape options.

Boarded Up/Abandoned/Foreclosed Houses: Already boarded up. Make sure there are plenty of exit routes.

Average Everyday House: Not boarded up, but more options in terms of multi-levels, exits, and accommodations. Since the power will be out, don't worry about finding one with a heated pool.

Recreational Vehicles: Great for travel, but not very secure. If you absolutely must, be sure to snag a new one, brand new wheels, no engine troubles, lots of bedrooms...a bar...

Generally, you'll want to avoid anything with plate glass windows, one level, and limited escape routes. Do consider anything with two or more floors, anything with an easily accessible attic which allows you to pull the stairs up behind you, and anything that you can defend with the people in your band.

Another option is a flat-roofed building as long as you can get onto the roof from inside the dwelling. Feel free to make the necessary modifications, especially if it isn't your house. The flat roof gives you the second-level escape option and enables you to use fewer resources for security. One or two people on a flat roof can adequately monitor the slow-moving hordes of undead sniffing their way to your position.

For those of you staying put because you were born in that house and you're going to die in that house, consider developing a network of Safe-Houses.

This involves nothing more than finding safe places to shelter in the event you can't get back to your main facility. Perhaps you find an untouched convenience store on Main Street.

Much like a child in the X-Box store, you lose track of time and before you know it, it's dark out and no longer safe to travel.

You calculate that it'll take you twenty minutes to get home, but only five minutes to get to Safe House two…Safe House two is now the smart choice.

Or perhaps zombies are knocking on your front door. You sneak out the back and escort your family to Safe House three.

You can always do what I've done. I live in a tractor-trailer bunker that I buried in the backyard.

Options keep you safe. Each safe house needs to be secure, but it only needs basic supplies. Food and water for a couple days, a change of clothes, some bedding, a weapon or two, and some basic first aid supplies.

Ways to Dispatch Zombies

Rural areas will inherently have fewer zombies to fend off than cities will. Why? Because there were fewer people living in rural areas to become zombified when the virus hit. Do yourself a favor...move to the country.

Once there, you'll still have to dispatch the zombies you find. You can't afford to let them propagate their own kind. Fortunately for you, there are only a few rules to learn:

1. Destroy the brain;
2. Cut off the head;
3. Break the neck.

You'll find that altitude and climate will have little effect on your enemies. Zombies don't breathe, don't sweat, won't dehydrate, and don't shiver. Freezing may slow them down a little more, but they'll have to snap off a frozen leg before the cold impacts their mobility. Think of zombies as the dead and human equivalent of a shark. All they do all day is eat. Doesn't matter if they just ate a half hour ago, they're ready to eat again the instant they see or smell food. You wouldn't cut yourself, dangle from a thin wire over the ocean, and think you're safe. You won't be any safer moving to the top of a mountain or the middle of a desert. Vigilance is your only protection.

That said, there are some natural obstacles that your zombies won't be able to overcome. Quicksand, deep snow, avalanches, wildfire...all of these may not kill your zombie friends but they certainly will slow or incapacitate the unthinking and undead. Remember that zombies don't have higher reasoning...sharks can't figure out how to get out of a cage until the gate is opened, and zombies can't figure out how to get out of quicksand.

Unfortunately, these obstacles can also incapacitate you. If you are using them as traps or defenses around your stronghold make sure you know where they are. Signs are OK...zombies can't read.

No natural obstacles on your street? Dig an old-fashioned dead fall. Once the zombie is inside you can dispatch him with a quick bullet to the brain. Just don't let the pit get too full. Even a zombie is smart enough to climb out of a hole on the bodies of his dead brothers and sisters.

If you're lucky enough to live by the ocean, feel free to draw the undead into the water. Why? Do they swim? Not really, but they may be able to slap around on the surface for a while. That's really a good thing, because that will attract the real sharks, and they will quickly and efficiently clean their living space of any carrion they happen to find in the water. That you rang the dinner bell can be your personal revenge.

Do not draw zombies into your fresh water supply...while there are plenty of fish who'll enjoy the snack, they simply won't work fast enough. The zombies will simply sink to the bottom and walk out, perhaps with fewer fingertips but their teeth will still be in place.

In the meantime, the quickest, easiest way to rid your neighborhood of an unwanted infestation is extermination. Back to the rules.

1. Destroy the brain.
   Use whatever is handy. Bullet, arrow, shovel...survivor's choice. Bullets do make noise and

subsequently may draw more zombies to your location, but if you're pressed for time, get rid of the one in front of you quickly and then get back in your car and move away.
2. Cut off the head.
Think D'Artagnan. Get a sword. This will require you to get a little closer than you may be comfortable with, but if your weapon of choice in the first rule was a shovel, you're an adrenalin junkie anyway. Knock yourself out.
3. Break the neck.
This requires you to get too up close and personal for comfort. You could be bitten or scratched so only do this if your gun is empty or your sword is stuck in some other zombie's spine.

Yes, you're going to be bone tired in no time. It won't be very difficult to knock off your first hundred zombies, but you're going to get damned sick of doing it. Try to remember that they don't feel it, and that you must 'do to them' before they eat your gizzards.

There is hope, however. Zombies continue to decompose after zombification. Until their flesh and bones break down to the point where they will no longer remain assembled, they will simply eat. But once their limbs begin falling off, all you'll have to worry about is avoiding their gnashing teeth.

Since the walking dead won't have been embalmed, the bacteria eating away at their bodies could have your zombies in pieces in as little as a few weeks. Unfortunately, anyone they bite or scratch becomes a zombie, sort of like a giant pyramid scheme. You could have to wait months, perhaps years, before you don't have to worry about them anymore.

Let's Talk Zombies

You may ask, "What started the Zombie 'Pocalypse?

I would answer, "Does it matter?" The age of Science is gone. No one will sit around and debate who started it...well, maybe they will, but what difference can it possibly make? You're not going to find them, and you won't be able to punish them...stop wasting time thinking about it.

What you need to know is that they can't be reasoned with and they eat human flesh. They do not run, though they can be excited by the smell of food. They do not intentionally pack or herd together, though the same smell of food will draw them from all directions and give them the facade of deliberate herding. Use the image of a shark feeding frenzy to get the idea. Once amassed as a group, they will begin to move from one aroma to the next en masse.

The larger the group, the more likely you will not survive an encounter with them. When the zombies in your area begin to resemble crocs at the wildebeest crossing, it is time for you and your group to move on.

Zombies have hearing second to none, and their sense of smell is heightened. They may not be able to smell you from a mile away, but if you are in the same neighborhood with one, it won't be long before you know where he is. He will follow the noise until he gets close enough to sniff you out.

Once you are found, the predator hunting you will only be thwarted from his task of consuming you by his own permanent death, or by you getting far enough away. He will continue to track your scent until it dissipates. Your smell can linger longer than you'd like.

Fortunately, if you are in your vehicle, you will be able to leave those particular zombies behind. Unfortunately, the problem renews itself the minute you find a new place to roost. And no, your car will not block your scent. If it won't float in a lake, then it isn't air-tight.

Let's Talk Zombie Jokes

You won't want to hit post-apocalyptic times without being flush in the humor of the era. Study these well. Make up more as you go along.

"How many zombies does it take to change a light bulb?"

"Fifteen. Their arms keep falling off."

"Why did the zombie cross the street?"

"Because the road pizza was fresher on the other side."

"What's the best way to serve a zombie?"

"On a plate with an apple in your mouth."

And let us not forget the ever popular fat and ugly jokes:

"Your Momma is so fat she could feed Zombie Chicago for a week."

"Yeah, well your Momma is so fat she could have six zombies chowing on her leg and not even know it."

"Oh yeah! Well your Momma is so ugly the zombies think she's one of them."

Food

Just like the zombies, you will also need food. If we're talking Zombie 'Pocalypse or a virus that killed most of the population, then head on down to your local grocery store.

What foods do you take?

- Rice
    - All of it. Minute, Uncle Ben's, Carolina, instant, boil in the bag, old-fashioned…don't discriminate. Rice lasts, like, indefinitely, as long as you keep it dry and it can keep you alive, like, forever.
- Root vegetables
    - We're talking potatoes, carrots, beets, turnips, onions, yams…anything whose fruit grows underground has a longer shelf-life than anything that grows above. Why? Don't know, don't care. But everyone knows that a potato sitting on the kitchen table for a week will be in perfect condition, and a head of lettuce left on the same table for the same time will be slimy and brown.
    - Cabbages may last a little longer than other leafy produce.
- Anything in a can or jar.
    - I say this knowing that lima beans and mushrooms come in cans and jars. Buck up…they will keep you alive if nothing else is available.
    - All the canned meats, even the sardines, will keep you in animal-based protein.

- Almost anything in a box or bag.
    - Make sure you can keep the box dry. Don't discount the danger of moisture on a box of pasta.
    - A cellophane bag won't be affected by moisture as long as the bag remains intact. Consider storing them in something sturdy, like a cardboard box.
    - Bread is in a bag, but it won't last long unless you can freeze it.
    - Bagels will last a little longer than bread.
    - Dehydrated milk and long-term storage milk come in boxes, and there is always something comforting about a nice glass of milk. Add sugar to dehydrated milk to improve the flavor.

What foods don't you take?

- Frozen foods
    - Unless you've got a running freezer, ice cream, Tombstone pizzas, and Eggos can rot where they are. There's no reason to bring them home and watch them rot at your house.
- Fresh produce
    - We've already discussed lettuce. The same goes for tomatoes and most fresh fruit. Of course, if you like brown bananas then go for it.
    - If you have the ability to can fresh produce, do so.
- Fresh foods

- Cheese can last a long time, and if it turns green you can just cut the mold off. After all, that's how many cheeses are cured, right? Unfortunately, when most fresh foods turn green, that's a good sign that you shouldn't eat them. Some foods in this category are hamburg, hotdogs, chicken, pork chops, lunchmeats…you get the idea.

On the other hand, if you are sheltering-in-place (that's code for staying put) and you are running a freezer, consider packing it with all the fresh meat it will hold. Skip the ice cream…as much as you'd like to have it, you will get more benefit from the protein.

Besides, snacks are snacks. You may not be able to salvage the ice cream, but potato chips come in bags…

But a grocery store has tons of other useful and not so useful things for survival. How do you wade through the items and make intelligent choices? Well, that's what you're reading this book for.

What other things should you take?

- Bleach, but only the unscented, regular, old-fashioned, leave-white-splotches-on-your-blue-jeans bleach
- First Aid supplies
    - Alcohol, peroxide, bandages, antibiotic ointment, analgesics
- Vitamins
- Soap and personal hygiene
- Razors and razor blades

- Batteries. Your AM/RM radio might not work, but you can keep your two-way radios, walkie-talkies, and battery-operated conveniences working.
- Candy bars.
    - Why? Because nothing feels better than comfort food. Ditto for brownies, cookies, and anything else full of fat or sugar and that you shouldn't eat in quantity. But right now, there's no one left to tell you that. Knock yourself out. Feel free to name each calorie you consume.
- Fire starting materials
    - Pre-fab logs, lighter fluid, matches, charcoal briquettes, cigarette lighters and lighter sticks, candles. Use batteries and steel wool if all else fails.
- Coolers and ice cubes
    - It won't last for long, but you can salvage a half-gallon of ice cream or two. It'll also give you some short term storage for fresh meats. Cook these first because the ice won't last long.
- Pots…so you can boil even more water at one time.
- Paper plates, cups, napkins
    - Saves you time so you can boil more water
- Plastic forks, spoons, knives
    - Ditto

"What about the environment?" you ask. Really? Dude, hasn't it already gone to hell in a hand-basket?

What other things should you leave behind?

- Hair dye. It'll suck to lift your freshly-dyed head from the sink to find a zombie staring into the mirror from behind you.
- Electric appliances. If you have a generator and you need an electric knife to carve up those venison steaks, then go for it.
- Candy Corn…no redeeming value.
- More than one carriage of household cleaners.
    - You do need to have some cleaners, but you don't need to fill up the house with them. Save the available space for food.
- VHS tapes
    - Don't try to record your experiences as a video journal. Despite the wonderful movie it'll make, anyone in your party who tries it will be the first one eaten.
- Furniture polish
    - You'll be too busy boiling water to worry about what's happening to your coffee-table.

Expiration Dates

We've all been brought up to throw things away when the expiration dates hit. However, food has become a precious commodity for you so you might want to rethink that.

A 'best if used by' date, is exactly what it says…the food inside the box, can, or jar will be 'best' if used by the date stamped on the package, but will still be edible after that date.

A 'sell by' date tells the store when to pull the item from the shelf. You certainly would prefer to buy something before that date and the quality may be diminished after that date, but it is still edible anyway.

A 'guaranteed fresh' date refers usually to fresh baked items. This is fairly easy if you think in terms of Dunkin Donuts. A donut made today is guaranteed fresh today. It is not guaranteed fresh tomorrow. If you buy it today and take it home to eat tomorrow, it will not be as fresh as when you bought it but you can still eat it.

A 'use by' date is pretty much the same as the 'best if used by' date. The date references the freshness or quality of the food, not whether or not it has spoiled and is inedible.

An 'expiration' date is another matter altogether. That really does mean the food 'expires'. Eat it at your own risk.

Other things to consider are:

- Distorted cans can be a sign of botulism
- Dented cans can have split seams, cracks, or holes that let bacteria in
- Bugs in pasta, rice, flour, or other grains does not make the food inedible
- Unnaturally green food is risky
- Anything that does not smell or look the way it should (green beans that smell like dead frogs or ham that is brown) could well kill you
- There are few circumstances where road pizza is a suitable side dish
    - The only one that immediately comes to mind is field dressing an animal that you hit with the car. If it ran into your tire and died without rupturing its bladder or intestines,

then go ahead and field dress it. When it doubt, just leave it.

One final thought on the subject of food...all calories should be viewed as friendly. You're fighting to survive. Dieting will diminish your ability to function. Potato chips, Pop-Tarts, Devil Dogs...anything that fuels your engine is acceptable.

A Random Thought About Nutritionists and Other Health Nuts

While I will agree that the healthier you are the more apt you are to outrun Chomper and his pals, I dare say you'll need more than three ounces of salmon on a nice bed of lettuce to fuel the activity.

Parents, much as you've been trained to feed your kids proper meals, these are the days that you want your kids up and moving quickly, not dragging their butts and blankets around as they wake up slowly over the course of hours.

To that end, think Hershey's and full-leaded Pepsi...juice them up and watch 'em run. Another option would be something full of complex carbs with some protein and fat thrown in for good measure. I doubt you'll have time to cook eggs, black beans, or quinoa...go with the candy bars. In fact, run behind your kids so you can continually pass more chocolate up to them as they run out of steam.

And if your troop happens to be *blessed* with a nutritionist who does nothing but harp on you for your eating habits, use her health to your advantage. Let her run point...you'll have time to change direction when the zombies find her first.

But...There's No Food Left

So, you were the last to get to the Big Y and there's nothing left but hair dye and VHS tapes. Don't fret. The food hasn't run out; you just have to look harder and in more places.

Let's not forget that you're apt to find a convenience store, either stand-alone or part of a gas station, around every other corner. Pharmacies, restaurants, bars, discount stores, K-Mart...they will all have food.

If the hordes of survivors have managed to hit them all and have taken everything from Twinkies to cow brains, you still have options.

See all those empty houses? Open the door, dispatch any zombies inside, and raid the kitchen. Again, the fresh foods are a mostly useless find, but nearly every American household will have canned or boxed foods.

If each household has a week's worth of groceries, and two-thirds of that was fresh or frozen, then the other third of a week is boxed and canned. If there are a hundred houses in your neighborhood, you end up with thirty weeks' worth of food.

Don't settle for that. Every time you leave the house, whether to go to the creek for water or out in search of gasoline, take time to stop at a house or two and add the boxes and cans to your survival pantry.

Unfortunately, if the disaster you face leaves more than a handful of survivors, there may be no empty houses. Millions of you will descend on the grocery store and only twenty of you will get out unscathed with a box of Hot Pockets.

Start planting, hunting, and fishing. Learn how to turn crickets and grass into a St. Patrick's Day stew because the days of plenty are over.

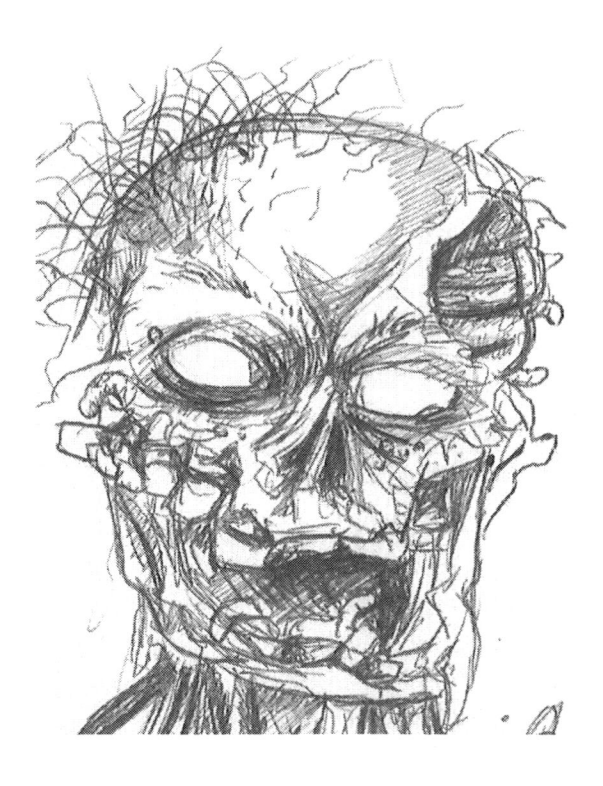

The Go-Bag

A Go-Bag is the backpack or other case that you grab when you have to beat a hasty retreat. Even if you plan to shelter in place, make sure you have a go-bag for every member of your band and any domestic animals you haven't cooked for protein.

The idea behind a Go-Bag is to provide basic survival needs. To that end, pack these items:

- A flashlight…don't pretend you are the Statue of Liberty and wave your torch around like a beacon as you scream "Give me your tired, your poor. Your huddled masses…" Use it frugally even if you have plenty of batteries.
- A sword, collapsible or otherwise, or a really large hunting knife
- A complete change of clothes, including shoes
- Food and water for three days
- Medications
- First Aid supplies
- A gun would be nice, just don't put one in the six-year-old's bag. Ditto for the bullets.
- A tarp or heavy, plastic sheeting
- Rope or cording

There are extra things you might want in a Go-Bag if you are facing a disaster other than the Zombie-Poc:

- A battery-operated or solar radio so you can keep tabs on emergency updates. Extra batteries are important, too.

- A two-way radio/walkie-talkie for calling for help. A whistle will do if nothing else is available.
- Respirator or dust mask for dusty conditions; a scarf is better than nothing.
- Spare cash in small bills…nobody will have change for a hundred, even if you do buy a pack of gum.
- An ordinary knife will do…skip the sword. The local school acting as emergency shelter will not think kindly of you for arriving ready for a ninja attack.
- List of phone numbers. Don't rely on your cellphone to work unless you have a place to plug in your charger. A list of numbers lets you call your brother, your Uncle Joe, and your Baby Daddy…anybody who can lend you a hand or a place to stay during the emergency.
- List of allergies to drugs, food, or other stuff. If you end up unconscious in the hospital, you don't want a double dose of penicillin if it's going to shut down your lungs.
- Copies of insurance and ID cards. No one is going to trust that you are who you say you are.
- Spare specialty items. Think eyeglasses, dentures…that sort of thing…anything you can't live without if you lose it.
- Toothbrush and toothpaste, and a bar of soap. They're small enough to fit even if the bag is already full.
- Extra keys to your house and vehicle. You may not have time to hunt yours down while you are running for your life.

If you only have one Go-Bag, DO NOT leave it the car…what happens if you can't get to the car? A central location in the house is perfect, perhaps an open foyer that you must pass through no matter which door you're headed to.

Unfortunately, you can never know from which direction the attack will come. Safety dictates having a second Go-Bag in the car or a secured location that you can be reasonably sure of reaching.

"But I don't have a real Go-Bag!" You don't need one. Use a backpack, small suitcase, duffel bag, or even a grocery sack…grab and go, that's the value of a Go-Bag.

Fire

You absolutely must be able to start a fire. If you can't master this skill, you will not be able to boil water, cook food, or stay warm. If you are counting on just using your generator, keep in mind that it uses fuel and I'd bet good money that you don't have a gas tanker in your back yard.

Matches, lighter sticks, cigarette lighters...you know the score. Flammables go on the bottom and you light them. This may seem ridiculously simple, but five out of ten people cannot start a fire and keep it lit on the first try. Repeat attempts will eventually be successful, but you don't have enough resources to waste. Learn to get it right on the first try.

Scrunch up newspaper, paper towel or leaves into a loose ball, stack up dried grass or thin brush, or rip apart something clean, dry, and made of cotton...pocket lint will do, as will a tampon. This is your instant combustible. Have more solid fuel like little sticks and even larger fuel in the form of bigger sticks ready to go.

The instant combustibles go on the bottom...light them up. Fire needs a gentle air source, so blow softly on the fire if it doesn't spark right up. Softly is key...this is not a birthday candle that you're trying to put out.

As this flame ignites, give it the small sticks a few at a time. Do not smother it! Nurture it until it gets bigger, and then feed it the larger sticks. When it's going on its own, give it a log or two. Air continues to be important, so if it looks like your fire is going out, rearrange the logs to let more oxygen into the flame.

There are also several designs you can employ. Practice with them until you find the one you can do quickly and efficiently.

- The teepee frame involves setting your instant combustibles inside a teepee frame of sticks roughly as thick as your thumb. This has your medium-sized fuel on hand already and gives the fire something to feed upon without waiting for you. Leave the door to the teepee open so you can light the fire.
- The cabin frame begins with two parallel sticks. Connect the tops of both with another stick; ditto for the bottom. You have formed a square, but the four sides are not on the same level. The discrepancy in levels allows air to pass through the sticks to feed the flames. Continue building the cabin until you are happy with the size. There is no definitive height. Set the instant combustibles inside the cabin and light.
- Overachievers can try the teepee/cabin combo. It allows air flow while keeping lots of fuel on hand.

If you have difficulty starting a fire on more than one occasion, consider keeping your fire lit at all times. It is not necessary to burn a forest to keep a fire hot; even small fuel will feed a fire. If the fire goes out, add more fuel and fan the coals briskly. You should be able to get the fire to ignite relatively easily, even after several hours.

What happens when you run out of matches, lighter fluid, and charcoal? No, do not eat the fish you just caught without cooking it…you'll get worms. But you do need additional skills for starting fire.

Here's where the steel wool and batteries come in, but you have to work quickly. Have your instant combustibles handy.

You can use a single 9-volt battery, or two D, C, or AA batteries stacked in a column. Rip a piece of steel wool off the roll, and pull it into a six-inch length about a half-inch wide. Touch the steel wool to both contacts of the 9-volt battery, or to the bottom and top contacts of your stacked D, C or AA batteries. The steel wool will begin to glow and then combust. It will not burn for long, which is why your tinder has to be close and ready to go. Shelter the burning steel wool with your hand if necessary so that any wind caused by movement doesn't put it out.

If you happen to come across a sportsmen shop, you can probably find a flint. It will also probably have instructions for use. If it comes with a magnesium block, that's even better. The gist of it involves shaving magnesium off the block...call it magnesium sawdust...and then striking a spark into the magnesium. The flame with be quick...have your instant combustibles ready.

Instant combustibles are most often referred to as "tinder." Once you know what you're doing, feel free to change the terminology. However, when you become a teacher of fire skills to everyone in your neighborhood, be sure to use the term "instant combustibles"...it is so much more impressive.

Almost anything can be used for fuel for this fledgling fire. But if you plan on using it for warmth or cooking, then dry materials are best. Green wood (for laypersons this means not-dried) will smoke considerably. Household furniture will kill you...the varnish and paints with which they are covered will create noxious fumes. You'll pass out fairly quickly, but you don't want to wake up to find a zombie on your leg.

One final thought on fires: don't build a bonfire so you can roast your weenies from twenty-feet away. Like your mother used to say, "What are you doing? Heating the great outdoors?"

Instead, build a small fire and get closer to it. It will require less fuel, make less smoke and draw fewer zombies.

The pictures that follow demonstrate the basic premise while assuring you that absolutely anybody, including me, can erect these structures.

Simple Cabin Frame:

Teepee frame:

Combo Frame:

Trees

In conjunction with fire comes the inevitable cutting down of trees. Your first temptation will be to cut down every tree nearby and use it for firewood. On the surface that sounds good and easy. You should reconsider. A little planning now will save you grief later.

If you plan on growing crops, decide where the field will be. If there are trees in the middle of the perfect flat patch of south-facing land, cut those trees down first. You take out two problems at one time…clearing your field for planting and stocking firewood for the winter.

The average person has no idea how to cut down a tree. With luck, one of your companions will have done this before. If not, prevent accidents by keeping everyone away from the cut zone.

You do have options: climb the tree or don't.

Without the availability of climbing gear, the branches will be your ladder. Climb as high as you can safely go. You don't want to climb so high that you will kill yourself if you fall out…a tie-on rope will keep you in the tree. You also don't want to stress the treetop so that it breaks under your weight…even a tie-on rope won't save your butt if the trunk snaps ten feet below your position.

So, now you're in the tree, and you've gone as high as you dare go. Chainsaw or bow saw…whatever your choice, be careful with it. If you slip, the saw slips, and off goes a limb. It's all fun and games until somebody loses an arm.

Top the tree...cut the top off and let it fall to the ground. As you climb down the tree, cut the branches off.

You can also buck the tree as you go...bucking involves cutting the trunk into manageable sizes. Do this all the way to the bottom and soon enough you have no tree, just firewood.

The problem with this process is the lack of professional climbing gear and inexperience in dropping trees in this manner. If you do not cut the top properly, it'll fall in your direction and squish you flat on the way down.

For a novice, I'd recommend dropping the tree intact while you stand on terra firma. First, examine any existing lean to the tree...it'll be easier to drop the tree in that direction than to fight gravity.

Next, determine your escape routes should the tree do the unthinkable...not do what you want it to do. If the trunk twists, it's not going anywhere near where you expect it to go, so you better be able to get out of its way.

The notch is the most important cut...it's a narrow V or a mouth-shaped cut that wedges out a notch one-third of the diameter of the tree. Place the notch on the side of the tree that is falling first...the side of the tree that represents the direction in which the tree will fall.

The final cut is the back-cut...this is the straight cut on the opposite side of the notch. For novices, place this cut a couple of inches above the notch to minimize kickback when the tree begins to fall. And now just stay out of the way.

Once it hits the ground, buck and limb it...cut off the branches and cut the trunk into manageable pieces. Trunks get split, larger branches become logs, but even the smaller twigs are good for kindling. Nothing goes to waste.

Just because the field is clear doesn't mean you'll never need wood again. Harvesting the rest of the trees in your yard will be easiest because they are closest to where your fireplace is, but doing so will leave you unbearably warm in the summer and at the mercy of winter winds.

Every tree in your ex-neighbors' yards, however, are up for grabs.

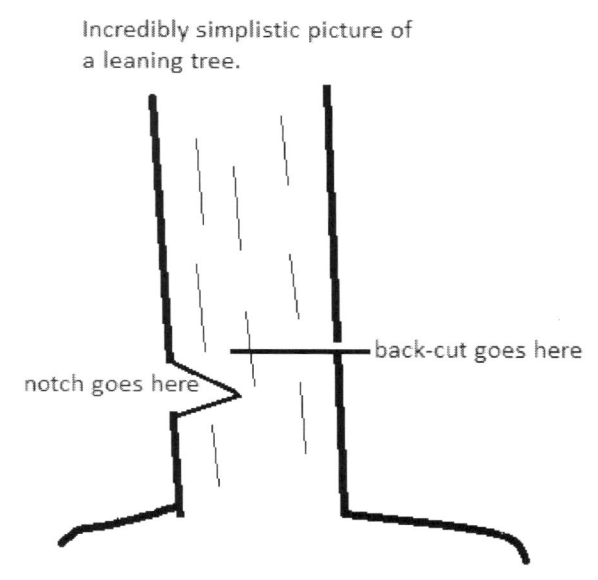

Incredibly simplistic picture of a leaning tree.

notch goes here

back-cut goes here

Gravity due to the lean and the carefully placed cuts make the tree fall toward the notch.

Building Shelter

This section pertains to those of you moving to Kentucky, Alaska, and the myriad places in between where you think maybe zombies won't have reached. I'm thinking the bayou, but wherever you go you'll need protection from the environment and the things in it.

Rule 1: Stay in a pre-built shelter if at all possible. Everything we've already talked about tells you to find a strong building, multiple floors, and no big windows.

Rule 2: Nothing ever goes the way you want it to.

You'll run out of gas or the car will die fifty miles from anywhere, and suddenly your options have run out.

Rubbish, I say! You still have options...you just need to know what they are.

Forests

If your car happens to throw a tire in the northern forests of Canada, you're surrounded by trees. That will be your best protection. You can always build a small shelter at the base of a fir tree, pulling the branches down and forming a nice little tent for yourself. Leave one side open...the fire you build outside the structure will heat your cubby nicely. But it will also allow predators in...not the four-legged kind because they will be afraid of that fire. The two-legged ones, on the other hand, don't give a rat's hoot about the flames because they've forgotten what it can do to them.

Instead, think vertically...climb the tree. Unless you've got some serious balancing skills, tie yourself to prevent rolling over in the night and dropping fifteen or twenty feet before you actually wake up. Don't knot the rope...you need to be able to untie it quickly if a zombie figures out how to climb.

To thwart such climbers, you need to pick a sturdy tree close to other sturdy trees. Climb only fifteen to twenty feet up, which leaves you nestling in among the thick, strong branches. Squirrels can jump from toothpick to toothpick, but you need something that can support your weight when you suddenly start tree hopping.

With any luck at all, there will only be the one zombie and you can simply dispatch him, which ends any concern you might have about your balancing skills as you leap Tarzan-like from tree-to-tree.

Of course, we've already established that you have no luck, hence the flat tire in the middle of nowhere. And no...you can't build a fire at the base of the tree. Yes, the heat will drift up to keep you warm, but so will the flames that ignite the tree bark. Imagine yourself as a giant sparkler spewing sparks into the night, with hundreds of pairs of undead eyes watching the show, their eyes all aglow with the promise of barbecue...

Mountains

Climb. Do not take shelter in a cave...limited escape routes. Besides, you can't hide in the dark. Zombies don't need to see you to follow the pungent aroma of fresh meat.

Find a ledge with an overhang. Zombies will not be able to reach you from above without falling off the mountain face. Use some of the rocks scattered around to build a wind break. One layer thick will suffice and still be light enough for you to push over if you have to escape.

Deserts

It's flat, hot during the day and cold at night. You can see what's coming from miles away, but they can also see you. Digging a hole in the sand will not save you...keep moving or kiss your butt goodbye. Hmm, I'm seeing a pattern here for you desert dwellers.

Other Considerations

On the off chance that you do have luck and it isn't zombies that destroyed the world, you may indeed have need of a shelter that is sturdier than the afore-mentioned.

Back to Trees

Yes, tie yourself into one. Or pull the branches of that fir tree down to form a small tent. Water and snow will run off such a structure and keep you dry for quite some time.

You can always seek shelter in a hollow log, provided nothing else is already living in there, snakes and skunks for instance. The small space will be easy to warm with your own body heat if you plug one end. Crawling in backward will allow you to drag something in to plug the opening in front of you. Unfortunately, should something decide to come in after you, you don't really have any recourse but to fight your way out. Zombies aren't the only predators capable of doing a job on you. Ricky Raccoon will be more than happy to rip off a couple of your fingers.

If your Go-Bag has a tarp, you can use that for shelter. It's waterproof, will block the wind, and will help keep your body heat in a small, confined area. You can even huddle beneath it if you don't have time to build a frame.

Erecting said frame is fairly easy, however, and there are dozens of designs. Quick, easy, and sturdy keeps you alive. Drape your tarp over a rope tied between two trees…instant tent. Stake the edges down so that the wind doesn't blow it around while you're trying to sleep.

Small tarps can be used to make lean-to shelters. Instead of draping the tarp over a rope, secure one edge to the rope tied between two trees and stake the other edge to the ground. Same principle as the tarp-tent but not enclosed. It'll shelter more people should you find yourself with three people and only a four-foot tarp.

As an extra challenge for you over-achievers, build a teepee. Take three sturdy branches and tie them in parallel line at one end. Once together, you can stand them up and form a tripod. Add additional branches to solidify the walls, and then wrap your tarp around it.

Keep your teepee small enough that your tarp can get all the way around. Secure one edge to the teepee frame but leave the other edge free so that you can come and go as needed and block out the weather.

If you decide to build a fire, build it outside your shelter and far enough away that you don't melt the tarp. Use rocks as a deflector behind the fire so that the warmth radiates toward you. When you decide to turn in for the night, bring some of the hot rocks into your teepee. Notice I said 'hot rocks'; notice I didn't say 'burning embers'.

Tent   lean-to   teepee

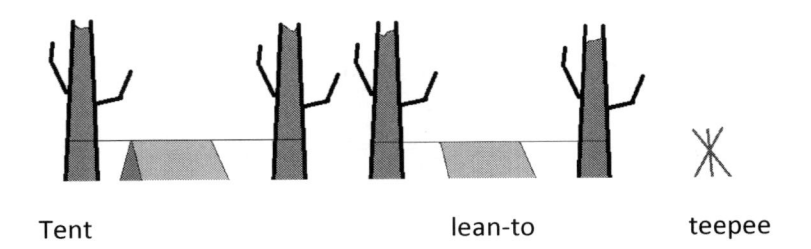

No tarp? Use lots of branches, preferably with their greenery still attached, and approximate these designs. No rope either? Gees, dude...go back three chapters and read the section on what you should have put in your Go-Bag. For now, use your shoelaces, your belt, any ties on your backpack, or a really long branch that you can wedge between two trees and use to hold the smaller branches in some semblance of a tent or lean-to.

Back to Mountains

Now you can take up living in a cave, provided it is not the day-bed of a puma. Small caves are better because you can heat it with less fuel. Large caves are better if you don't like your travel companions.

Back to Deserts

I suppose you could dig a hole in the ground and then pray that it doesn't collapse on top of you. Of course, every cold-blood creature will be drawn to your body heat...rattlesnakes, scorpions, and the like...yeah, there really isn't a lot of help for you.

Who Owns the Stuff

For those of you who are law-abiding citizens, you'll need a little prodding. All that stuff...the empty stores, the empty houses, the vehicles parked in front of the Lexus dealer...all that stuff belongs to whoever takes it.

There is absolutely no reason to fill a box truck with plasma TVs and haul them to Alaska with you. That space is better used storing food. Of course, if you are staying in your home and will spend the evenings watching DVDs, feel free to get that ninety-four inch TV that covers an entire wall. Do keep the surround-sound down, however. No need to advertise your position to the local undead.

Help yourself to whatever helps you survive the disaster. But if someone shows up and says the John Deere you're driving is his, then give it back. Lawn tractors are lying around unused at every other house...just get another one. Don't get killed over something that can be replaced.

Given the advent of *really free* markets, take caution not to become a car collector. You've always wanted a '67 Mustang, and your neighbor isn't using his anymore. But then it becomes an obsession and you end up with a Corvette from every year they were made, a Ferrari, a Lamborghini...and the field you were supposed to plant with crops is now a parking lot.

Do have cars stashed around with supplies in them, preferably hiding said vehicles in garages so that casual passersby don't drain the gasoline out of them. Skip the four-cylinder economy cars. Yeah they're great on gas mileage, but you need something big enough to drive over whatever happens to throw itself into the road in front of you.

Need a new axe, chainsaw, lawn tractor? NO, I don't mean now! After the zombies take over the world…if so, then take them. Your survival depends on it. Take the food, the water, the weaponry. You might only be able to shoot one gun at a time, but you'll need roughly three-hundred-fourteen million bullets…one for every American-turned-zombie.

Odds are that only half a million of us will be smart enough to avoid infection. If all the survivors get together and split the work, that means each of you has to pick off just six-hundred and twenty-eight undead. I don't include myself in that number because I live in an ocean-bound houseboat…the sharks will take care of any zombies that come looking for me.

Gasoline

Generators run on gasoline, but gasoline pumps run on electricity. When the power is out, you're going to have to work for that gasoline, just like you work for your water.

You have to ask yourself if it's worth running a generator when zombies have hearing second to none...we've already discussed that. But if it's just a common virus and you don't have to worry about attracting the hordes of hungry undead to your home, then you'll need to know how to proceed.

If you happen to be traveling to Fort Knox, don't waste time trying to crack gas tanks at the local Cumberland Farms. Get a syphon from a K-Mart, Wal-Mart, or auto parts store, and syphon the gasoline out of any parked vehicle. Don't bother with cars on the street that have open doors, or that crashed into telephone poles. Those ran out of gas because some half-wit zombie wasn't smart enough to turn the car off.

But if you are sheltering-in-place, the tactics are different. Sure, harvest the gasoline from your neighbors first. Then hit the stores and get all the gas cans you can find. Finally, go to the closest gas station, find the keys, and open the tanks. If you've got a long enough and strong enough syphon hose, get cracking. Otherwise, you need to find a small container that will fit through the fill hole. Lower it via rope.

When you're done filling your gas cans, lock the tanks back up and take the keys with you. Sharing is nice, but you're responsible for your family now more than ever before. If somebody stops by your house and you want to give them some petrol, by all means do. But you never want to find out that some militia passing through drained the tanks and left you high-and-dry.

Now, gasoline won't last forever. You can always get fuel stabilizers at the auto parts store that will let you keep the gasoline for up to two years, but sooner or later that gas won't be any good. It will make your equipment start with difficulty and run roughly. And eventually, your equipment won't start at all.

Should you choose to use your generators, despite the fact that they will draw zombies to your door, you've got a two year clock running on your gasoline use. The gas in the station's tanks will go bad, the gas you've stored away in your shed will go bad, and you'll end up with nothing on which you can run your gas-powered generator.

All hope is lost.

Or is it...?

Go down to Lowe's or Home Depot and get yourself a propane-powered generator. Propane lasts indefinitely in a sealed tank. The tank, however, usually has a shelf-life...ten years in many jurisdictions...which is designed to keep consumers safe from leaky or faulty equipment.

To test a twenty or forty pound tank, take it down to your local watering hole and submerge it. If there are bubbles...the tank is shot. Do not attach it to anything and try to use it. You will BLOW YOURSELF UP.

To test a hundred pound tank, do the same...just have somebody on hand to help you.

Day to Day Living

Rise, shine, check the weaponry. Make sure it is in working condition, properly oiled and cleaned. Fill your magazines (those little things that hold the bullets) or cylinders (that twisty, twirly thing on a six-shooter). And keep that bad boy on your person at all times. Do not get caught in the john with your pants down and a zombie in the shower.

Breakfast. That doesn't change and every bit of normalcy adds to your sense of well-being, keeps you grounded, and makes you forget that someone wants *you* for breakfast. Eat a good breakfast when possible, but do not gorge. You are still fighting for your life, but you may not be able to stop for lunch. Keep snacks handy.

After breakfast, it's back to work. It's down to the watering hole to get today's supply. It's boiling it all and storing it all, and making sure you have plenty of hydration. Water's most important so it has to be first.

Gasoline comes next so that those of you running generators don't lose any food. Of course, if you're not running a generator you won't need gasoline for that use, but you may still need it for tractors and tillers and chain saws, all equipment that will help you survive by plowing up land for planting crops, and cutting up the trees to burn for warmth and cooking.

You'll also need gasoline for your cars and trucks. Keep those tanks full and start them daily, even if you are not planning on going anywhere. Plans change quickly; you don't want zombies banging on the windshield when you figure out the car won't start.

Speaking of cars...don't hang onto a vehicle for sentimental purposes. The '67 'Vette might be fast, but it won't hold enough supplies to make a difference. The car you had in college and kept because you lost your virginity in it is going to break down sooner or later. That classic, fully restored El Camino might look great sitting there with a For Sale sign on it, but it's still better than fifty years old. And the truck with the slipping transmission will eventually strand you someplace.

The minute you suspect your vehicle is no longer trustworthy, dump it. There are plenty of vehicles sitting in driveways and parking lots. Take them. Find one that suits all your needs...mega-cargo capacity and appropriate seating. If you want a sunroof, go for it. If you want a trailer hitch, knock yourself out. The point here is to keep yourself in reliable transportation so that you never get stuck having to elude zombies on foot.

Lunch. If you can stop for lunch, do it. Something quick and light to take the edge off. If you're traveling, take the opportunity to stop for a half-hour to stretch, pee, relax, and enjoy being alive. Then get back on the road or back to work.

Now you have houses to raid, stores if you can find them, and resources to add to or replenish your survival supplies. You need to do this whether you stay put or caravan your way to Kentucky.

For those of you sheltering-in-place, you must also tend your crops and animals if you have any. Farming is a full-time job in itself. This is one of those tasks which will be easier with a larger band of survivors. However, if your fields aren't enclosed by fencing, you also need armed guards whose sole job it will be to protect the field workers.

The evening meal. You can't have it yet. It has been moved to later in the day. Before you get to eat, you must secure your safe-house or wagon train.

For caravans, take the time to circle the cars and trucks. Use them as your protective wall. It worked two-hundred years ago, and it will work now. String together tin cans on wire and put them farther out from your vehicles. This early warning system will immediately draw your attention to any approaching zombies who aren't smart enough to step over the wire. However, if land-pirates are approaching, your clever booby-trap does nothing...you still need armed guards at all times.

Armed parties can gather wood for a small fire, then do a head count and make sure everyone is accounted for. If you are missing someone, do not holler at the top of your lungs to find them. If the zombies have them already, they'll soon have you as well. Small armed parties can go into stealth mode to search for the missing people, or you can write them off as zombie snack food.

Now you can eat your final meal of the day. It should be substantive to keep you comfortable through the night, but not so heavy that you can't escape a sudden onslaught of the undead. Do not eat a pound of pasta, or it will be your last meal. On the other hand, if someone in your band does eat a pound of pasta, stay close to them. When the zombies overtake him or her, they'll forget all about you.

For home-dwellers, walk your perimeter. Secure any loose doors or windows, check your booby traps for gaps in coverage, and double-check your weaponry. Do the head count. If everyone is paying attention, then anyone missing is still inside the compound. If they were dumb enough to leave in search of Twinkies without telling you, then I would leave them to their fate. Whether or not you do that depends on your circumstances. If the missing person is your mother-in-law, your life may be better in the long run if you lead the search party.

Sleep. Rotate guard shifts every four hours, more often if your guards can't stay awake. It won't help you to post somebody for a four-hour shift if they're going to sit down and sleep the minute everyone else is snoring.

And it starts all over again in the morning.

The Family Pets

Fido and Fluffy have always been part of the family. If they survived the initial infection without catching it, then they are still with you in a condition that you can handle.

If, however, your dog, cat, cockatoo, or goldfish goes for your throat, don't dismiss that as a bad dog day. If he's chained to a tree and has the links stressed to the max as he tries to reach you, he is not agitated. He is Zombie Dog.

Do not try to save 'turned' family pets. Much as you love them, the most humane thing you can do for them is 'put them down'. Explain to little Bobby Joe and Sally Sue that the loving, loyal animal that once slept in their bed will no longer protect them. Better yet, just euthanize the animals while the kids sleep and tell the youngsters the animals ran off.

But if you are fortunate enough to have animals that still behave like family pets, you still have problems. Let's discuss these animals in the order of popularity. Sorry folks, but more cats are owned as pets than dogs. Most likely this is due to apartment dwellers who can only have small, quiet pets.

Cats

Of those U.S. households that own cats, just about half own a single cat. The other half owns two or more cats. Cats are loving, don't take up a lot of room, can pee in a box, and don't make a lot of noise. They won't attract zombies by barking every time a bird flies by.

Here's the dilemma: they are easily frightened, will run and hide rather than stand their ground, and rarely come when called. You may have the exception to these generalizations, but every cat I have ever called needed an incentive to respond. "Breakfast is ready!" is a good one, or "Who wants snackies?" Shaking the canister of treats usually brings them, but it will be just a tad inconvenient to run through the house dodging zombies, grabbing your Go-Bag, and shaking the treat bottle as you try to figure out where Fluffy is.

A cat left behind is likely to become a snack. If you cannot retrieve the animal before bugging out, then at least leave a door or window open to give the animal a fighting chance. If the zombies follow you, and your kids won't stop crying, come back in a day or two to see if the animal survived.

Dogs

Of all U.S. dog owners, most own a single dog, about a quarter of dog owners have two dogs, and the rest own more than two dogs. Dogs are also loving, and they can be fiercely loyal and protective of their owners. Unless they are particularly stubborn, most will come when called, and anything but a Rat-dog can carry its own Go-Bag.

Here's your dilemma: they must go outside to pee and once there they may well bark at everything they see...this is an instant invitation for zombies to check out the ruckus. Unless you own Chihuahuas or other Rat-dog varieties, they take up a lot of room in the family car which limits the amount of supplies you can carry. And if you are under attack, your dog is going to want to make a stand. Think about when your dog disregards your wishes the most...yeah, that's right...when he thinks he's saving your butt and you're not smart enough to know it.

A dog left behind also becomes a snack for the zombies. He can't hide under the dresser like your cat can. If he refuses to respond when you call, you must leave him behind. Certainly leave a door open in case, but he doesn't have the mobility a cat would, and he isn't likely to escape.

Birds

They're cute, spend their lives inside a cage, and are easy to transport. You can set them next to your Go-Bag and grab them on the way out of the house. The down side is they are trapped in that cage waiting to be eaten if you can't get to them. Depending on where you live and what type of bird it is, it may be more humane to just let it go.

If you're lucky enough to have a bird that you've trained to fly around the house, come to your whistle and land on your shoulder, then you are all set.

Mice

Or hamsters or gerbils or any little rodent type creature, excluding Rat-dogs...

In an aquarium? Turn them loose. They are one of the few creatures that will be able to survive in the wild without any additional instructions. They eat just about anything...grain, cardboard, wood...they'll be fine.

In a cage? If the cage is small enough, then treat it like a bird.

Fish

The tank weighs too much to grab-and-go, the water will slosh around the vehicle during a high-speed escape, and the little buggers will die of stress anyway.

Just eat 'em.

Or set them loose.

Or throw them at the zombies...maybe it'll be enough of a diversion for you to get away.

Turtles

Boxy owes no allegiance. He looks happy to see you because he knows you are the bringer-of-food. Just turn him loose.

Rabbits

Chances are the cage is too large to be easily moved. If you can stand it, eat the little beast. Otherwise, turn him loose.

Snakes

Really? This creature will never return your kindnesses and certainly doesn't need your help to survive. Turn it loose. If you're really worried about Mr. Slithering, turn loose the food crickets you keep in the other aquarium.

You cannot discount the emotional value of a pet. It brings you joy, comfort, relieves stress, and gives you something to focus on besides your personal struggles and problems. That's why we keep them around.

Your choice is heart-wrenching...hope you can keep them with you and safe, turn them loose to fend for themselves, or watch them die horribly. I don't envy your decision, but I do have the decision myself. I expect the dog will be the first one to go because she won't shut her yap and she won't listen…stupid Rat-dog. I expect the tomcat will be the second to go because he loves people. He isn't smart enough to know that dead people aren't the same as other people.

The two female cats will hide under a bed somewhere…they'll be just fine. And it won't be long before they find the open door. That's when their struggle for survival will begin.

I'll swing by in a day or two to round them up…after all, I live in a recreational bus with flame throwers strapped to the sides.

Crops

Zombies or no zombies, your life will depend on your ability to find food. Don't wait until you run out of canned and boxed foods. Begin planting as soon as you find a safe location.

What should you grow? Well, don't bother with something you won't eat. It's a waste of time. And don't spend a lot of time with frivolous items like strawberry corn. You need food, not gourmet popcorn.

Another consideration is yield for the amount of work involved. Consider that asparagus grows a single stalk, but a summer squash can grow dozens of fruit.

So, what should you grow? Here's a list with my personal experiences included. Whatever sounds like it might suit the bill should be added to your list.

- Corn
    - Super easy to grow, but anything in the grass family usually is. Some varieties grow a single ear, others multiple ears. The healthier the plant, the better the fruit. Corn needs a lot of water, however.
- Squash
    - Easy to grow, high yields, but susceptible to bugs. Hit a garden shop and pick up insecticide to make sure you get to keep those yields.
    - Many varieties break the boredom of growing only one thing. Zucchini, summer, acorn, butternut…the first two are best for

immediate consumption, while the latter two are good for longer storage.
- Tomatoes
    - Picky. If they grow well, you'll have good yields. If they do not flourish, you'll pour a ton of time and resources into something that won't repay your work.
- Potatoes
    - Another easy one. No doubt you'll have potatoes with eyes growing from them in no time, simply because you can't possibly eat all the potatoes you harvested from the grocery store. Cut the potatoes so that each piece has at least two eyes. Plant them eye side up.
- Cucumbers
    - Normally easy to grow but not much nutritional value.
- Strawberries
    - Will grow like weeds, will propagate themselves easily for many years of production, and don't need a lot of care. Just keep the rodents away from them and you'll be fine.
- Fruits trees
    - If there's already an orchard standing, feel free to harvest. However, do not spend a lot of time planting fruit trees unless you are skilled in that particular art.
- Peppers
    - Bell peppers can be tough to grow.
    - Hot peppers are easier to grow but few people sit down to a plate of them.

- Rhubarb
    - Pretty much a weed...you almost can't kill it, and you almost don't have to tend it.
    - Mix it with other stuff to improve the flavor unless you like it tart.
- Eggplant
    - Keep it well watered and fertilized and it will produce a lot of fruit.
- Cabbage
    - Can be difficult to grow, but once they kick into gear they will form heads quickly. Keep the bugs off.
- Cauliflower
    - Eager grower but susceptible to bugs. Use insecticide.
- Beans
    - Green beans, both pole and bush varieties, are quick to grow and bountiful in yields.

A root cellar will keep produce like potatoes, winter squashes, and corn for longer periods, but a lot of it will have to be preserved either by dehydration or canning.

Improper dehydration can lead to moldy and inedible food. Improper canning can kill you. Before you undertake these very important survival tasks, go to the library and get the appropriate books.

"Wait! This is the Zombie 'Pocalypse book! Just tell me how to can food and get it over with!" That's what you'll say.

My answer: It takes thirty-five minutes to hot-pack tomatoes, fifteen minutes to hot-pack strawberries, but twenty minutes to pressure-cook green beans. There are far too many variables. Besides, this is the Layman's Guide to Surviving the Zombie 'Pocalypse...canning vegetables is an advanced course that has already been written by *Ball*.

Common threads among the vegetables you decide to grow include feeding and watering the plants. You'll have ample choice of fertilizer...your local K-Mart will have tons of it. Water is the commodity that may elude you, especially if you are trekking down to the river every day. Make use of rain barrels when possible and recycle as much 'wash' water as you can.

A decision you will eventually have to make is whether or not to eat something that a rodent has chewed on. After all, it was just a nibble...

You are facing your own extermination. If the little rodent had rabies, he wouldn't have been nibbling on your veggies. He'd have been chasing you around the yard. Cut off the part he nibbled and cook the rest.

Another decision is what to do with half-rotten fruit. My feeling is that it is only half-rotten. The part that isn't rotten is perfectly good. Cut off the half-rotten and cook the rest.

Finally, since you won't always have access to Burpee seeds at the garden shop, you'll have to not only harvest your fruit but harvest the seeds as well. Save those half-rotten parts for their seeds.

Once the Zombie 'Pocalypse has passed and all the zombies have fallen into pieces that can no longer threaten you, spend some time creating an irrigation system. At this point, you can hook up a gazillion generators if you like because the zombies won't be around to hear them. Run all your neighbors' water pumps and divert the water into your irrigation system. Hardware stores, Home Depots and Lowe's will have PVC tubing for this purpose.

Also consider greenhouses. A generator and a heater will keep a greenhouse warm enough to grow some cool weather crops like cauliflower, peas, lettuce and the like.

Toileting and Other Uncomfortable Conversations

When the power goes out, the toilet in your home becomes a useless pit. It won't matter whether you live in the city or the country or whether you have public sewers or a shallow well and a septic tank, the juice is off.

No electricity means no pressure in public systems and no power to private systems. Flushing does absolutely nothing.

Bucket flushing will work for a little while. This involves pouring a vigorous bucket of water into the john to force the disposables out of the bowl. The principle behind this is that you are creating the pressure.

However, this won't work for long. The pressure you create is minimal, and the solids will begin to settle in the pipe, backing it up and causing you to eventually abandon your home due to the smell coming out of the bathroom.

Options are nearly endless:

- Porta-Pots are everywhere. Hooking one up to get it back to your house could be a problem, as will emptying it. But they have large storage tanks and will sit outside, keeping the stench out of the house.
- Camping style portable toilets. Easy to transport, the big drawback is the small size of the tank. However, they can be used indoors and will contain the smell if you use the appropriate chemicals. They are also small enough that you can take them outside, dig a hole, and dump the contents when the tank is full.

- Composting portable toilets have the same benefits as the camping style toilets above. The added benefit is that they compost the waste.
- Digging a latrine gives you a longer term solution. It is outside of the house, keeping the smell distant from your living spaces. It is, however, far enough away that running out at two a.m. could be problematic. You would also have to look inside the pit before settling in to read a week-old newspaper because a zombie could have fallen in there.
- Special lids are sold that fit five gallon buckets and turn them into portable toilets. The usable tank capacity is somewhat less than five gallons...you don't want to slosh waste around when you take the bucket out to dump it.
- And you can always squat like a bear in the woods

No matter what you choose, be sure to keep these waste products away from your fresh water source.

If that discussion wasn't entertaining enough, we have another topic to cover. Ladies, sorry...you cannot dispose of your 'personals' the old fashioned way. Wrap 'em up and bury them...deep.

When the World Goes Silent

We don't hear very well...none of us do. We get used to the noise that surrounds us.

The sounds of traffic are readily audible at three a.m. when you expect it to be quiet and you're trying to sleep. But at five p.m. when you get home from work, you don't grant the traffic a second thought.

At five p.m., when you want to get out of your suit and heels, when you want to sit down to dinner and a beer, catch a TiVo'd game, and forget that your boss is a complete butt-head, you completely miss the fact that a family of eighty-four sparrows has turned the space above your front door into a condominium.

But when the traffic stops, when the hum dissipates, when the world goes silent, you'll be able to hear a great deal more. The sound of machinery or an automobile will be heard from miles away.

You can either seek it out or hide from it. Rest assured that it won't be run by a zombie, so the living human on the other hand could be friend or foe. Go armed, ready to defend yourself, but without posturing or attitude. Do not seek a confrontation.

Consider that they are in the same boat as you are, trying to survive and not knowing whether you are dangerous or not. Taking supplies with you in an effort to trade will make you look less threatening to them and may give you a way to start that conversation.

Rules Of The Road

I know you...blowing through yield signs because you think that you can squeeze your twenty-foot long car into a ten-foot space between two oncoming vehicles doing eighty-miles-per-hour.

In fact, I've seen you do it. And I've given you the horn a couple times.

Don't worry...there's no reason for you to stop now. Having to actually yield to oncoming cars would mean that there were some oncoming cars. If you see them, yielding will be further down the list, somewhere behind heart attack and slamming on the brake.

As far as yielding to pedestrians goes, you best make sure those pedestrians aren't the decaying, hungry, unreasonable kind.

Stop signs will become the new yield signs. You'll slow down enough to make sure no one is around, but you won't linger long lest the zombies catch up with you.

Traffic lights will no longer be functioning...they went off when the power did. Still, don't assume you have the right of way. Keep your eyes open for movement.

School zones will no longer be a mandatory 'slow' zone...as if they ever were. You'll be teaching your kids at home, as will anyone else with a brain. No one is sending their unprotected offspring to the zombie buffet.

Yellow, white, solid, and broken lines are meaningless. Drive on the wrong side of the road if you want to…you've been doing it ever since you got that cellphone anyway. The difference is that now you don't have to worry about getting nailed head-on.

Turn signals will be nice if you're traveling in a caravan; otherwise you'll use too many calories to worry about telling no one that you're changing direction.

Speed limits have always been for whimps. Now that you can drive ninety down Main Street, you won't. You'll drive slowly for two reasons:

1. You're looking for supplies, survivors, and zombies
2. You no longer have to prove you can get away with speeding

If anyone comes up behind you with flashing lights, I'd suggest pulling over just in case it really is a cop. Keep the car rolling, keep it in gear, and keep your foot on the gas…just in case it really isn't a cop.

I also know those of you who will pull out in front of the only visible car on the road…apparently you have to get out there first. Now you'll be pulling out in front of the last remaining car on the road…consider the wisdom of that before you do it. They have no reason to stop anymore.

What To Do If a Zombie Is At Your Door

Question one: Is he/she alone?

- Yes
    - Open the door, shoot him in the head, and go back to your DVD and popcorn.
- No
    - See question two.

Question two: Are there too many for you to handle?

- No
    - Open the door, shoot them all in the head, and go back to your DVD and popcorn.
- Yes
    - Grab your Go-Bag, your bird cage, your family, and skedaddle, Pilgrim.

Your life in Zombie-ville will be ever changing. One day everything will be fine and the next day everything will go to pot. You must have options, your plans must not be cast in concrete, and you must be flexible.

What To Do if the Zombie 'Pocalypse Hits While You Are At Work

There is a thirty percent chance that the zombie-making virus will hit while you are at work, and a fifty percent chance that it will hit while you are not at home because all your free time is spent running errands, at the gym, or shopping. Too bad you never learned to be a home-body.

Your first instinct will be to get home. That's where your family and pets are. That's where your responsibility lies.

Problem is that they may think they need to get to you. If you do nothing else with this book, then make a decision right now with your family about who is going where. Are they waiting for you or going to you? If the house isn't safe, where will you meet them? Or are you all just staying put and dealing with the situation from the location in which you find yourself? Have these plans in place before a disaster hits.

For the sake of discussion, the decision is that they will wait for you at home. Grandma Gertrude's is the secondary meet site, and Uncle Joe's is the tertiary site. You leave work, expecting to hit the highway, do about eighty miles per hour, and be home in exactly twenty minutes and seven seconds.

And then you actually hit the highway at a screaming stop. Everyone thought the same thing. Your best bet may not be the highway. It may be the back-roads. Yes, it will take longer but the odds are great that you will actually be moving.

Extra caution is called for anyway. People will begin to do nutsy things...drive on the sidewalk, through yards, passing you in the bike lane in a Suburban. You will want to be uber-defensive in your driving skills. If somebody wants to get by you, just pull over and let them go by. Don't let them go all road-rage on your butt and drive you off the road. Later than expected is better than never arriving.

If the road becomes impassible...say one of those nutcakes causes a major accident that plugs a road...you will do what you know you must. You will do the nutsy things like driving through someone's lawn or on the sidewalk, or fording small springs with your Volkswagen Beetle. If the Beetle gets stuck, you may have to ditch it. Now you're on foot.

If you were around the house doing chores and what not, you'd be clocking in at around two-miles-per-hour. After all, you're not in a hurry...you're just doing chores.

If you were walking for fitness, you'd be pressing it, trying to get healthy, and pumping at three-and-a-half or four-miles-per-hour.

But you are trying to get home. You're going to be tempted to break into a run and charge up the street. Home may be around the corner...great. Or you may still be a half-hour from home. Thirty minutes in a car doing thirty mph means fifteen miles on foot. If you go off all stoked and hell-bent to get home immediately, you're going to run out of steam long before your four-hour walk is over. You'll end up adding more time onto your journey because you'll have to stop and rest.

Of course, if you're a marathon runner, knock yourself out. Most of us aren't marathon runners. A casual walk for the average, healthy person will be around three-miles per hour.

Do the math. Five hours at a comfortable speed gets you home. You've added a single hour to the trek without having to take a nap half-way home.

Once you get home, hopefully you'll find your family already boarding over the windows and loading the shotguns. Should you find the house leveled by a micro-meteor, head to site two. Odds are great the spouse took the car, which leaves you on Bobby Joe's bicycle. It'll be faster than walking. Now if you want to sprint, go for it because on a bike you can cover up to twenty-five miles in a single hour on a smooth surface.

If your family and Rover are at site two, great. Otherwise head to site three. Once you find them, put your emergency plans into action. Either you are battening down the hatches and preparing to defend the keep, or you are loading up your family and heading to Alaska. I hear there will be even fewer zombies there. I also hear that polar bears like zombie meat almost as much as sharks do.

Tons of Other Things

Fast forward to the time when the zombies have disintegrated into multiple body parts, only one of which poses any serious threat to you when it tries to bite your ankle as you walk by.

This is the time that you'll be able to band together in bigger communities, splitting the work and the rewards. The more people in your compound, the more crops you can grow, the more people you can support...and that's how society begins again. Everyone begins to calm down when they figure out there really is a way to survive without knocking off the few remaining survivors.

You can double your efforts in regard to hunting and fishing, and you can begin to raise animals for food...if just two of you managed to keep your pet rabbits alive, animal husbandry will soon have you knee deep in them. Somehow I doubt many of you will have had the stomach to eat little Billy's bunny for lunch so you'll likely be butt deep in rabbits.

If you can capture some chickens, you'll have eggs in no time. If you can find some cows (unlikely...they're almost as dumb as zombies) or goats, you'll have milk with which you can make cheese. When they get old, or sick, or stop producing...when they've outlived their usefulness...you get to eat them and make clothes from their hides. Harsh as it seems, that's the circle of life. That's the way your ancestors did it, and that's the way you'll have to.

At this point, you can freely go into town and raid the library. Look for how-to-books. How to garden, build a smoke house, dry foods, skin a deer, make cheese from goat milk, and don't forget that book on canning and preserving. Pick up some basic medicine books, but unless you really have a doctor on hand, skip the surgery books. I don't want you thinking that all you have to do is read up on it and you'll be able to perform brain surgery.

Also pick up fire-making books. Eventually all the batteries will be dead and all the steel wool used up. You'll have to know how to make fire by rubbing two sticks together, and you'll need to build a fire-carrier that will let you carry your embers and coals from place to place.

You really don't need Harry Spotter, but it will keep the kids amused, get them interested in reading, and let them be kids for a few hours a day. And when they've read all eighty volumes of Harry Spotter's adventures, you can always use them to start a fire.

What you do need are educational materials, books to teach the next generation how to read and write, to add and spell, and some basic history so that humanity's triumphs and tragedies don't disappear.

If you can't find some suitable books for the kids' education, hit a school. There should be plenty on hand and will most likely cover multiple grades/age levels.

Society is now yours to make of it what you will. You can use the experiences of our ancestors to rebuild in their image, or you can modify their design to suit current needs or improve upon any shortcomings.

Resurrecting civilization is something you probably want to do freshly showered with clean hair and teeth. Even though noise will attract zombies, they can't move that fast when the only moving parts are their jaws. Those of you with shallow or artesian wells are free to hook up a generator to your water pump. It will draw a lot of juice…twenty-five hundred watts minimum with a thirty-five hundred watt starting surge. That's about the average size of a generator you're apt to find at Home Depot or Lowe's so don't bother putting anything else on that generator.

You can, however, get as many generators as you want…line them up outside, build them a nice little shelter to keep the rain off or erect a bunch of umbrellas. DO NOT bring them in the house. Do run extension cords that are as short as possible to minimize output loss.

There are limits to the power output of generators. You can pick up a book at the library that will explain amperage and wattage and help you figure out how many lines and what appliances you can run from a single generator.

In the meantime, there are a couple simple items to know. Surge wattage versus running wattage. The 'surge' occurs when you first start something that consumes electricity. The wattage then drops back and settles into the 'running' consumption. For instance, a basic AM/FM radio without any bells and whistles will take 120 twenty or so watts to start up, but will then only require 70 watts to remain on.

Approximating usage requires plugging stuff in to see what happens. Start with a simple light. Plug it in and let it run while you plug in other things. If you want the fridge, plug it in. If you want the microwave, plug it in. If you want a portable heater, plug it in.

Now, I'll tell you that you've just loaded 4560 surge watts on that one generator, so it better be a big old boy. But its running watts are only 2760. The short of this example is that if you turn these items on one at a time, allowing the surge to settle into running mode, all these items will be able to run on a single 5000 watt generator if you can find one.

Of course, I can't possibly read your mind. Maybe you'd prefer the flat screen TV to the heater...after all, you can just wrap up in a blanket to watch DVDs of *I Love Lucy*. There's no way I can give you every combination of appliances.

So how will you know if you're pushing the limit of your generator? When one of the larger appliances begins to excessively draw power, running slow then fast repeatedly, like it's surging and draining, you've begun to stress the circuit. When the light bulb starts to do it, you are very close to your limit. And when the safety circuit on the generator triggers off, the generator is overloaded. Rework your attachments until you have smooth running of all appliances.

The electric water heater, however, will need 4500 watts all by itself. You'll need to decide if you want a hot shower that bad, or if you can live with a bath and buckets of water heated on a fire. Another option is unplugging everything else from the 5000 watt beast in the example above and swapping off with the water heater when you need it.

Which Disaster Shall It Be?

Who can possibly know?

Meteor, volcano, zombies, virus, EM pulse, the collapse of the Stock Market...the common thread is your survival. Any preparations you make now for any disaster-event will help you no matter which event happens.

Storing food? You'll need food if a virus hits, if the Market collapses, or if a volcano spews out enough ash to cut off all shipping routes.

Deciding where to meet up with your family? You need to know that whether a meteor hits two states over, a flood blocks all roads home, or a tornado blows through town.

Packing Go-Bags? You need those if a freak Halloween snowstorm takes out the electricity for a week.

Yeah, but will there be a disaster? It's only a matter of time. We've already taken the first step toward the Zombie 'Pocalypse with designer bath salts and people dumb enough to smoke it.

Nuclear fallout? Consider all the aggressive countries striving toward nuclear capacity.

The collapse of the economy? That's already happening.

Bottom line...it is never too early nor too late to take steps to help your family survive a disaster.

Steps You Can Take Now

- Prepare a Go-Bag for each car you own.
    - Make it yourself
    - or buy one ready-made at any of the emergency preparedness websites
- Learn to make fire.
    - Teach your kids.
- Learn to purify water.
    - Teach your kids.
- Set up your 'meeting' sites.
    - Make sure everyone can recite it from memory.
- Take your dog to obedience school.
    - Reinforce the training daily.
- Teach your cat to catch rodents.
- Stock up on extra food.
    - MREs (meals ready to eat)
    - Dehydrated
    - Freeze-Dried
    - Canned
    - Bulk purchases at Costco, BJs, or Sam's Club
- Buy a copy of this guide book for every member of your family.

None of these needs to be a major expense. For instance, you don't need to buy an expensive backpack for your Go-Bag. You can start with something as inelegant as a grocery sack. The clothes you put in the bag don't need to be brand new...old stuff you don't wear often is fine.

If cost is a major concern, the internet can teach you how to train your dog as long as you do it before the power goes out.

You can also begin your disaster storage by buying just an item or two extra at the grocery store each week...a couple extra cans of peas will only cost you a couple bucks.

The important thing is simply to start because if there is one thing civilized people agree upon, it is that we are in for major trouble in the not-too-distant future.

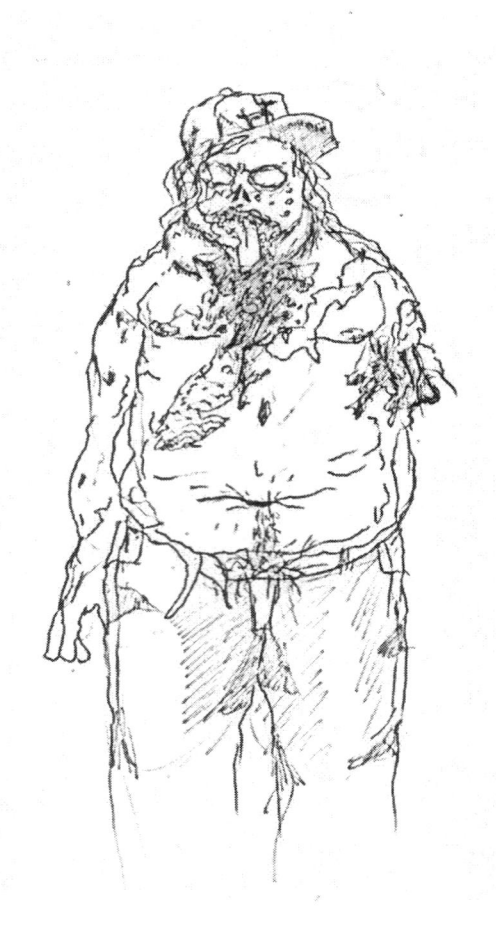

Finally

The world has gone to pot, the survivors have banded together, and life goes on.

Take the best of the past world and incorporate it into your lives. Leave the worst of the past world in the past and endeavor not to make those mistakes.

Color, creed, lifestyle choices...none of that matters anymore. We are all just people. We want to raise our families, protect our kids, want to benefit from the fruits of our own labors.

We thrive on our own generosity and willingly help those who cannot help themselves, but we revolt against those who would take advantage of our good nature.

We worship our God, or not, in the manner we choose. You are free to worship as you wish...I will not interfere. Do me the same courtesy.

All in all, remember that you few survivors are all that is left. The future of this world is yours to shape. You may not all shape your future in the same manner, but respect each other enough to rejoice in your diversity.

A Disclaimer of Major Proportion

I do not, nor have I ever owned stock in an MRE company, Smith & Wesson, or a manufacturer of Go-Bags.

I do not, nor have I ever had any inside governmental information that suggests that the Zombie virus is an inside job, designed by the Feds to control the populace.

Nothing in this book should be construed as resembling anyone that you might know. It isn't about your Uncle Joe or your Grandma Gertrude…it may seem like it at times, but trust me…I live in a remote cabin with no neighbors for miles, behind a twelve-foot tall concrete wall and a camouflaged metal gate. I don't your know your family.

And finally, you cannot hold me responsible for any damage that comes after reading this book. Why? Because this book is just a guide, and now that you know what you're facing, you should be preparing for the end of the world! Get cracking, Rookie!

An Open Call

Got ideas of your own?

Send them in. I will compile the best into ZP2. Now, if a hundred-thousand of you decide to take me up on this, I reserve the sole right to pick and choose between you. To that end, make your submissions so ingenious that I can't possibly ignore them, or make them funny as all get-out.

On the other hand, should only two of you actually read this far, I reserve the sole right to simply reprint this book with your ideas tacked in as appendices. Either way, you'll all (or both) be able to say that your work has been published.

"What will I get paid?" you ask.

"My undying thanks as you and I strive to save humanity from itself...literally," I respond.

Do keep in mind that while I am hacking a path through the zombie horde, I will not have time to respond to everyone individually. By sending in your ideas you agree to have them published in this manner. And I agree to give you all the credit so make sure you give me your name, Twitter ID, or other suitable handle.

I also promise to clean up punctuation, spelling, grammar, and inappropriate terminology without modifying the *true* meaning behind your creative juices.

"And how do I contact you?" you press, hoping to glean the secret of immortality that exists in the written word...

Ah, grasshopper...you have two choices:

- the forum at www.ZombiePoc.webs.com
- or the contact information at the front of this book

If You Enjoyed Zombie 'Pocalypse...

Go on Amazon and let me know. Your reviews will help spread the word; pretty soon there will be more survivors than zombies and we can get back to the business of living sooner.

Also check out this author's other works.

Tuesday's Child
This triple award-winning debut novel chronicles one teenager's struggle to survive abuse and homelessness.

Tuesday's Child 2: Redemption
The sequel illustrates the difficulties a once-homeless teen will encounter when trying to live in the 'real' world.

Haven
Soon to be released, Haven is a look into the future...
Global warming, global cooling, and a soldier just trying to get home.

Tuesday's Child and TC2 are both available on Amazon.com. Autographed copies make great gifts for your book loving family and friends and can be ordered from www.TuesdaysChildNovel.com on a first come-first served basis at a special price...provided I don't have to burn them for warmth...

Made in the USA
San Bernardino, CA
23 August 2017